MW01293554

Stairway To

Heaven

VICTOR HICKS

GOD'S MESSAGE OF LOVE

Crystal Stairway To Heaven: My Journey to Healing

Copyright © 2018 Victor Hicks

All rights reserved. No part of this book may be reproduced or transmitted in any form or by any means, electronic or mechanical, including photocopying, recording, or by any information storage and retrieval system, without permission in writing from the publisher. All questions and/or request are to be submitted to: 134 Andrew Drive, Reidsville NC, 27320.

To the best of said publisher knowledge, this is an original manuscript and is the sole property of author **VICTOR HICKS.**

Printed in the United States of America

ISBN-13:978-1983804427

ISBN-10:1983804428

Printed by Createspace 2018

Published by BlaqRayn Publishing Plus 2018

DEDICATION

THIS BOOK IS DEDICATED TO THOSE WHO NEED TO KNOW

John 3:17-

*That **God** did not send **His Son** into the world to condemn the world, but to save it.*

To those dealing with past trauma, depression, **PTSD***, inner wounds and betrayal*

Our Father loves you!

Also:

TO THOSE WHO HAD THE STRENGTH AND GUTS ENOUGH TO TELL THEIR SUPERNATURAL EXPERIENCES

GOD'S MESSAGE OF LOVE

NO MATTER THE COSTS.

ACKNOWLEDGMENT

First and foremost, I'd like to thank my Heavenly Father (Abba) God, who has been so gracious to me. Thank Jesus my LORD and Savior for His sacrifice and patience with me.

I'd like to thank my Parents Willie and Ora Hicks for loving me and teaching me to be honorable.

To my big sister Alice, who always encouraged me. I can't wait to see you again in Heaven.

To all my brothers and sisters, nieces and nephews who seem to believe in me more than I believe in myself. I love all of you.

To my beautiful children and grandchildren who I love more than I can express.

To my wife Joy, who always cheers my writing on.

To my niece Kneika, who inspires and encourages me.

Crystal

<u>Stairway To</u>

Heaven

GOD'S MESSAGE OF LOVE

<u>VICTOR HICKS</u>

<u>INTRODUCTION</u>

Youngsters can't seem to wait to grow up fast enough. Adults often times wish they could go back to their youth. The secret of contentment is elusive for some. Others never unlock its codes. Yet, some seem to be born with a satisfied disposition.

I was not one of the latter. It took me a couple of near death experiences and other supernatural encounters to find my way out of my emotional abyss. Hopefully this true story can be helpful to others who need to know how to receive the Father's Love.

Crystal Stairway to Heaven

As I opened my eyes in the emergency room, I looked up to see the doctor standing over me as I lay on the hospital bed. He exclaimed, "He's awake!"

I couldn't tell you what he looked like. My mind was still adrift I suppose. I was thinking about where I'd been. At the time, I didn't remember. I only knew something unusual had happened, something I couldn't explain. The only way I can describe it is, it was like I had been hollowed out and refilled with something else. I mean my insides; my soul, mind, heart, my spirit like stuff. It was like my innards were scraped out and replaced.

There really are no human words to describe how I felt, not from my vocabulary anyway. I was upset that I'd failed again. I was embarrassed that my family saw me like this. *Great*, I thought, *all of this and all I'll get is just another damn doctor bill*!

GOD'S MESSAGE OF LOVE

As my eyes scanned the emergency room again at St. Luke's Hospital in Kansas City, Missouri, I also saw my first ex-wife standing near the bed talking to someone who appeared to be a doctor. *What's she doing here* I thought. *This must've gone horribly wrong and I'm in hell...*

My name is Victor Hicks. I was born in Kansas City, Kansas in 1962. I am the tenth of 11 children born to Willie and Ora Hicks. I have seven older sisters. I have two older brothers and one younger brother. I also have two half brothers and a half sister. My dad remarried and from that union, I have three stepbrothers and a stepsister. Having these many siblings gave me an understanding, at an early age, of dealing with many different personalities. It also taught me empathy and patience with people. All of them had a different personality and perspective. Each had something to give. Sometimes something to take away. I believe this in-home training helped me with my career in law enforcement later in life.

I have worked in many different areas of law enforcement. I've spent most of my career inside the jail. I've encountered just about every type of human personality there is, I suppose. Growing up in my big family most certainly gave me a head start in psychological diversity. At the time of this writing, I was serving my nineteenth year as a deputy sheriff in my home town.

We grew up in a big white house, at least it seemed big when I was growing up, on Quindaro Blvd. The national news once called it the most dangerous street in America after one particularly violent evening when over 20 people were shot within the area of a few blocks. That was in the 1990s when rival gangs and the crack cocaine epidemic were at their apex. I was never involved in any of its activities; however, I saw many of my classmates, friends, relatives and neighbors go down because of it. Some lost their lives to shootings and other violence, some succumbed to drug overdoses, others to prison, and others lost their sanity. In my early childhood years, however, it was a fun, interesting, family oriented neighborhood.

Most evenings, my family and some neighborhood friends would sit on our front porch and talk, people watch and play games, but mostly, enjoy the evening breeze. In the sixties, we had no air conditioner. The cool night air and fans were all we had in the summer, but I don't remember anyone complaining about the heat, we were just thankful for the breeze.

The younger ones of us would play "hide and seek" and catch "lightening bugs" as we called them back in the day. My sisters, brothers and neighborhood kids also had relay races a lot it seemed. I was pretty fast, but never the fastest. My childhood was a normal childhood of sorts. I had my childhood crush. She was my neighbor (Cheryl) from across the street. She was 7 to 8 years my senior. If her front door slammed, I was more attentive than her dog. I'd be gawking out of the window at her. She was beautiful.

I didn't care too much for school as a child; I have never been a morning person and school started too early in the morning. When children are in kindergarten or first grade, the teacher normally asks what do you want to be when you grow up. The answer you give as a child, I believe, is what God has placed in your heart to be. I really believe that. Just like inside of every fruit seed is a small picture of that fruit. You can see it through a microscope. I wanted to be a police officer and I wanted to be rich as a child. That is what was inside my seed. I accomplished the law enforcement part. It took longer than I'd planned, but I became an officer. I still have that dream of becoming rich. At the time, I wanted money for the usual childish things. I wanted a big car. I wanted the biggest house. I wanted the prettiest wife. As I grew older, my priorities changed. I still wanted money, but I wanted it so I could help people. I wanted to be a secret Santa.

As a young child, I also remember seeing the photo of the little girl from Vietnam on the Time or Life magazine cover. She was burned, naked and crying after a devastating attack on her village during the Vietnam War. She was without anyone to pick her up or hold her. She had no one to comfort her. She probably had lost her parents and other family in the bombing. I wanted money to be able help that girl also. I don't know how money would have helped, but if it could have helped, she would have gotten it. I used to think "what kind of evil world is this?"

In the 1960s, we did atomic bomb and natural disaster drills in elementary school. This was such a frightening time for me. The nuclear bomb drills were the scariest. We would line up and walk orderly down into the dingy, dank school basement. I remember the musty smell, the dirt and cobblestone floors…oh, the cobwebs. Then we would huddle together in a corner or under a large object like furniture. We were taught that Russia was always close to nuking us and vice versa. I don't know about other people but they were very scary and traumatic times to me. Even today, when our local area tests the disaster warning siren, those same feelings of dread initially hit me. I live in Kansas City, Kansas where tornadoes are a very real threat.

I suppose that's one reason my young life was also plagued with depression. Maybe it was a foreboding of impeding doom. I never could place a finger on the direct source of my sorrow. I didn't even realize until I was much older that everyone else wasn't perpetually sad, too. I didn't realize I had an issue. As a matter of fact, I didn't understand that I had lived a depressed life until I was in my 40s and did some reflecting. Later in my life I would learn the reason why.

To my family and friends, I'm a comedian and a fun-loving guy. I can be the life of any party. I never wanted to bring anyone else down with my maladies so I never shared my emotions with anyone. I especially didn't want to bother anyone with problems whose source I couldn't put a finger on myself. No one talked much about depression or mental illness when I was young. You dealt with it the best way you knew how.

I also remember being hungry a lot in school as a kid. I don't know why I was so hungry. We had enough food at home. I recall reading "The Cat in the Hat". I used to think *I'd eat green eggs and ham*! On a boat, with a goat, on a train, in the rain… I'm still hungry most of the time fifty years later.

My dad and mom divorced when I was 2 years old. I was so young, I never actually remember my dad living with us. He later moved about 3 blocks away on the same street; where he owned a candy/grocery/pinball game store. He was not a man who could work in a normal job setting. He was a businessman and as far as I know, he never held a so called "regular" job. My brothers, sisters and I worked in his store cleaning and stocking shelves. When we were big enough to reach the cash register, we learned how to operate it. My school friends thought we were rich because he owned the store; not hardly. We struggled financially like everyone else in our neighborhood. However, there were some perks to having a store.

We got to enjoy the pinball machines, pool tables and games before everyone else. Video games and equipment are common now and pretty much taken for granted. In the sixties and seventies, that was not so. When I was a child just seeing a pinball machine was magical. There was always a line to get to the flashing lights on the machines. I remember the bings and pings as the pinballs shot around the top of the game. It was kind of like a tiny Las Vegas with all the flashing lights. My dad and his new wife, Jessie, lived in an apartment directly above the store. My stepbrothers and sister lived with them.

My father was a 33rd degree mason. I never knew what that meant but I knew his companions revered him. He was respected and well known in the black community of Kansas City, KS in the 1960s and 70s. As I understand it, he was also partial owner of a dry-cleaning business and an ice cream shop. He also owned several other stores later and a body shop. He was a very smart man. He couldn't understand why everyone couldn't pick up on his conversations. He had traveled the world while serving in **World War II** and **Korea.**

Whenever he talked about his involvement in the wars, he would speak of it in the third person. He would say, "I know a man who did such and such…" He never told us that man was himself. I see now this was his way of coping with the horrors of war he surely encountered. No one knew or talked about **PTSD** or any war related trauma back then. You just dealt with it the best way you could. Back then, we just dealt with many things the best way we knew how.

I remember one story he shared with me of soldiers who had been captured during one of his tours of duty. The captives were placed in metal tanks of water with their hands secured outside of the water tanks in a cross like position. Inside the tanks were small octopuses that would latch on to their legs and lower body to torment the captives. He had many stories of war in Italy and Germany and other places. He expected us to know about the places he would describe. He was educated before America started dumbing down its education system. He was very smart with more than a genius **IQ,** I'm sure. He expected us to catch on to what he was talking about or teaching. Like when he taught us how to count back money from the cash register. We were 3 and 4 years old, but we learned it. He expected it. I thought everyone knew how to count change back when I was younger. Almost no cashier can count back money these days.

When he died in his early 70s, my sister looked through his vital papers and we found out he had been a **Prisoner of War** and was the recipient of a *Purple Heart*. We, his children, were totally unaware of any of this. He was also an avid reader when I was a child. He seemed to have given up on reading later in life.

He was a man you did not sass or talk back to. He had no patience for disrespect; he held firm to a zero-tolerance policy in that area. Disrespecting someone around him could possibly result in a butt whooping. I thank him for those lessons now. In my career, respect is treated as currency. He taught us how to give honor to others and respect people regardless of their position in life. Elders were Mr. and Ms. or Mrs., also ma'am and sir. It didn't matter if they were homeless, penniless or if they had mental issues or whatever. They were respected by us in front of our father... or else.

He and my mother didn't go to church together. He wasn't much of a church person. One evening though, he came to our church, I don't know what the occasion was. Maybe one of my older sisters was singing or one of his children was in a church program. Whatever the occasion, I remember in the middle of the service, the door opened and daddy walked in. I don't know why but I was so happy to see him. I can still remember it like it was today. It was fifty years ago, and I can recall the suit he was wearing. I was overjoyed to see him at church with us. I ran over to sit by him. That was a happy evening for me.

GOD'S MESSAGE OF LOVE

My mom raised us alone pretty much, save for the help from my elder siblings. She had the mothers' way of making each one of us her own special child. So, since I'm writing this, I was the favorite. She worked in the kitchen at KU Medical Center until she retired. She was a genius at reading people. She could tell by a persons' gait whether they were worth the time of day. I didn't fully understand her wisdom until later in life. It would have behooved me to have learned it earlier. She was a very funny woman and an excellent cook. She would make this yummy buttery rice pudding. I wish I had paid attention to the way she made it. I'm still trying to replicate that recipe.

My son had a dream once where he saw her in Heaven. She was still cooking desserts there and smiled at him. She also taught us to pray and to fear God. She made sure we went to church and vacation Bible school. She loved to hum and sing. Most of my siblings and their children sing as they go through their days even now. We got that from her. She would sing while cooking, driving, cleaning or just hum when she would sit on the couch with her eyes closed as she rocked back and forth praying and as I understand now, she was probably meditating. I had no concept of meditation as a youngster. Lord knows she needed it with eleven kids. We also took in friends of my brothers and sisters to live with us from time to time, along with relatives who needed shelter in our home. Many of them are like brothers and sisters to us until this day.

My oldest sister Alice (Al), was like our 2nd mother. She was also the family organizer, coach, encourager, prayer warrior, among other good things. I say "was" because she passed away in April of 2011 of a heart attack at age 62. I remember thinking, while I was at the hospital the day she died, *what in the world are we going to do without Al?* She was also an angelic singer. She made several gospel albums with different singing groups and choirs. She was a school teacher; she retired Friday and died Saturday afternoon.

I also lost two other sisters, Ora "Renee" and Ruthie. Both died of illnesses in their 40s. Renee left 2 young sons and a daughter. Ruthie left behind three young daughters. Both sisters were very creative. Ruthie in home decorating, writing and humor. Her children and grandchildren are similarly gifted. Her daughter, **Kneika Robbins,** has had several books published.

Renee, on the other hand, was also very humorous but very serious about education. She was the school spelling bee champion for several years. She also was an excellent teacher and nurse, who created fun and exciting ways to teach us how to learn and remember concepts. She would create songs and rhymes to help us remember various school lessons and spelling. She taught all the younger brothers, sisters, nieces and nephews to spell their names with creative songs and jingles. I still remember those songs almost fifty years later. Of course, they both loved to sing.

All my siblings are very smart, geniuses even. They are self taught computer experts, published authors, playwrights, mathematicians, valedictorians. Some have photographic memories, others are entrepreneurs, etc. All except me. The girls in the family got their college degrees. I have always wondered why God left me out of the family talent pool. Aside from being able to crack a few jokes, I could never think of a thing I was good at. I was okay at several things, just never found anything I was very good at. This vexed me most of my life as I tried to find a niche, a calling or something I was even passionate about.

CHILDHOOD

My mother spoke of God often and prayed at home. She took us to church, Sunday school and vacation Bible school. I didn't understand church much. I liked our early childhood, Pastor Rev. Banks, at the Antioch Baptist Church. He was passionate about what he was preaching even if I didn't know what he was going on about. He would get very animated in his sermons. He would shout, pant and point, sweat and cry. He would set the church ablaze with "Amens" and "Hallelujahs". The music was great in our congregation, especially when my eldest sister Al would sing. I was so very proud, even as a very young child, to see and hear her sing. She always sang to God with passion and emotion.

I had no particular interest in church as a child. I liked the big, unusual words the preacher used during the messages. I had no earthly idea what he was talking about, but I loved hearing the long words with four and five syllables during sermons like tabernacle,

Nicodemus and Nebuchadnezzar. I didn't know or care anything about the Soul etc., I just listened for long words. That's all I remember about the messages. I recall being upset because I had to get up so early for what amounted to foolishness to me at the time. Yes, I thought church was foolishness when I was young even though I believed in God and I knew He was a personal God. I was never into church; I'm still not. I remember being hungry a lot in church too.

I don't remember my exact age but while I was still in grade school, Rev. Banks passed away and Rev. Stephens became the new pastor. As in any emotional situation of that magnitude, there was difficulty accepting the change among the church members, but I liked the new pastor. I liked him mostly because every Sunday, Rev. Stephens seemed to love the big words and names as much as I did. He seemed to always mention the tabernacle. He would also sprinkle in a few Nebuchadnezzars for good measure. Yeah boy! However, the biggest event in my spiritual youth is when my brother and I went up front for the alter call. The alter call was usually at the end of the service when congregants were invited to accept the Christian call. I was about five years old and my brother was four. I still remember it today. We just got up and went up front with no prompting, coaxing or coaching. I don't recall any change that happened in my life. I already believed in God. There were no lightening bolts. I didn't see any angels descending. So, I went on with my childhood life. We were also baptized at the church not much later.

To my recollection, the closest encounter of anything of the spiritual and supernatural realm came from our neighbors next door. These were not good spiritual experiences by the way.

Mr. Cline was in his own words a "warlock", his wife Rose, a "witch". I didn't know too much about that sort of stuff back then but I have since found out they thought it was very real. These people were very serious about their witchcraft.

Our neighborhood was all black except for those two. They hated us and called the police 10 or 12 times a week if we looked in their yard. We would kiss any baseball, football, etc., before we went outside to play with it because if the ball went in their yard, it was gone. They would stab the ball with a knife if it was an air ball or take it into their lair, never to be seen again. Therefore, we'd kiss our footballs and basketballs goodbye before we started playing just in case. They claimed to have cast evil spells on all of us. They owned dozens of cats and kittens, and, I swear at night the cats would call our names in creepy, scary, feline voices.

When Mrs. Cline passed away, Mr. Cline started talking to us. He apologized for his years of malicious behavior and blamed most of their horrid actions on his wife. He died soon thereafter. When he died, his brother came over to clean out the house. He found homemade voodoo like dolls made in the likenesses of our family members in their house. He showed them to us. We also believed, and still do, that our house was haunted. I never saw anything in the house out of the ordinary, but I heard a lot. I would hear bumps in the day and night. I heard stairs creaking and strange voices. However, my family members saw entities, people etc. Recently, on my family's Facebook page, we discussed our past strange occurrences in the old family home. Several family members mentioned the hauntedness of it. They talked about hearing unexplained voices, footsteps and other assorted creepiness.

<u>HOMELIFE</u>

I suppose my home life was normal for a kid growing up in the sixties. Like I've said, I was the tenth of eleven children in the home after all. My mother and dad divorced when I was two years old. Mama raised us with the help of my elder siblings.

My mother would go to work by city bus early in the morning and arrive home by bus late in the evening. Most of us would be there at the bus stop waiting for her. Often, she would bring us snacks from work like ham sandwichs or chocolate cookies. The younger kids, (me included) would hang onto her skirt (literally) and follow her around the house until she scooted us away. We could hardly wait for her to get home from work. The older siblings would cook and make sure the house was presentable.

As I look back now, I always remember having an underlying sadness in my heart. I never knew why. My mother told me later in my life that I had a very bad reaction once as a young child to aspirin and strawberry soda. Also, she told me of another terrible allergic reaction to penicillin.

After having read accounts of other people's near death experiences or **NDEs,** I never knew anyone who talked about or wrote such things until I was nearly fifty years old. I wonder if I'd had an **NDE** during one of those allergic episodes. I understand with some people, once you've had a taste of eternity, you are not satisfied with the temporal. I don't know for sure, just my theory.

As I write this, no one who was around at the time is alive to be able to tell me. I just know I carried a burden of sorrow continually.

I am now and have always been known as a comedian. Most, if not all comedians, I've learned in life, deal with depression. The comedy comes out of inner pain mostly. One of my favorite comedians of all time was Johnny Carson. I watched his show every night as a young man. One day, as he neared retirement, there was a television special on his life. I was amazed and surprised to find that he wasn't the happy-go-lucky guy portrayed on the Tonight Show. He was a shy recluse. He battled depression and other demons like anyone else. That was an eye opener for me. It was the first time I saw maybe we had more in common than I had originally thought.

While I'm on Johnny Carson, I have sort of a personal story. Once when my 1st wife was still in high school, she had a friend who needed a liver or kidney transplant, can't quite remember which one. The operation would cost around 100 thousand dollars. The whole high school and parts of the city, got involved with raising money for the procedure. We had bake sales, car washes, rummage sales etc. At the end of it all, I believe we raised about 40 thousand dollars, sixty thousand from our goal.

One night while I was watching television, I thought I'd write and ask Johnny Carson for the rest of the money. After all, he seemed like a great guy. I made a copy of the newspaper article concerning our mission and fundraisers then attached a letter. I made 10 copies or so and sent them all to Johnny Carson in Burbank, appealing for help. He sent me back a response stating he can't give out money like that because everyone would be beating down his door and he can't help everyone as much as he'd love to, which was understandable to me. However, someone unanimously donated 60 thousand dollars right before the deadline. No one will ever be able to tell me it wasn't Johnny Carson who donated that money. God bless his soul. Our friend had a successful operation, by the way, and was as cantankerous as ever afterward.

I spent most of my childhood playing alone with toys or ants. I had friendships but I preferred being alone. If I did play with anyone, it was usually my younger brother Dwight. I watched a lot of TV. Gilligan's Island, Astro Boy, Johnny Sokko, Speed Racer, Flintstones and others were among my favorites. I had normal TV crushes like MaryAnn on Gilligan's Island and Catwoman. I pretended to be Hayata on Ultraman. I wished I could get my afro to bounce like Jackie Jackson's did when he danced or that I could sing like Jermaine Jackson.

In my seventh-grade year, I had my first serious, steady girlfriend. She was the prettiest girl in Kansas City too. Senora Richardson was her name. When she told me she liked me, I started shaking like Don Knotts in the movie "**The Ghost and Mr. Chicken**". She thought I was funny and cool while it lasted. When she broke up with me, I couldn't eat for days. I was too young to be that serious anyway. However, she sure was beautiful.

Events like this in my life would awaken the melancholy monster dwelling in the dungeon of my soul. I wondered if all my relationships would be like this. I was sure others felt bad when relationships ended. When you're that young, you don't think or care about anyone else's problems. I heard the poem in school by Langston Hughes called **Mother to Son**; this poem often reminded me of the sorrow and frustrations in my life:

Well, son, I'll tell you:

Life for me ain't been no crystal stair.

It's had tacks in it,

And splinters,

And boards torn up,

And places with no carpet on the floor --

Bare.

But all the time

I'se been a-climbin' on,

And reachin' landin's,

And turnin' corners,

And sometimes goin' in the dark

Where there ain't been no light.

So boy, don't you turn back.

Don't you set down on the steps

'Cause you finds it's kinder hard.

Don't you fall now --

For I'se still goin', honey,

I'se still climbin',

And life for me ain't been no crystal stair.

Throughout my own life, as my depression worsened, I would add my own verses to this poem.

Life for me ain't been no crystal stair

–fact it's raining, raining everywhere.

Is anyone listening? Does anybody care?...

Why must my soul be laid bare?

.   .   .   .

No one talked about depression when I was young. When I was older, I thought it was a weakness. It's very real and a tough one to battle. As I write this, my full-time job is a deputy sheriff. In our profession, there is so much depression and alcohol use and abuse. Everyday you run into broken families, betrayal from friends, backstabbing, backbiting, hatred, spouses cheating, fighting, abuse, ridicule, scorn, divorce and then we go out and deal with the public. Law Enforcement is always in the top 3 in suicides yearly. One year, law enforcement was beat out by dentist. What's that all about?

An average of 22 military veterans take their own lives in the United States everyday. We all hear about the high-profile suicide cases. Professional football player for the San Diego Chargers and all around great guy, Junior Seau's, suicide really hit me hard. I loved that guy. How could you not love Junior Seau? I heard maybe it had something to do with the concussions football players are so prone to incur. I remember seeing his beautiful mom on TV in so much grief. That really tore me up. Of course, Robin Williams's suicide touched nearly everyone.

One of my dearest friends from the police academy recently ended his own life, which was a complete shock to most who knew him. We were supposed to be meeting for lunch around the time it happened. I wish he had let someone know of his pain, or at least allowed someone to help him. Most men try to deal with this illness on their own. If you're dealing with depression, please seek help immediately!

Anyway, back to my childhood. I really don't have too many standout events. I never really liked school. I was never a morning person. I'm still not a morning person. I did fairly well in spelling, geography and history. I was very small in stature growing up. I received the usual meanness from kids in school about my looks and clothes. I say *usual* because it seems most everyone was ostracized and teased to some degree. My family wasn't rich, so many times my clothes stood out. I was a fighter though. We didn't have bullying seminars back then. Even though I was tiny, I'd fight if I had to.

I didn't reach 5 feet tall until the summer of my pre-senior year in high school. I weighed less than 100 lbs. I wanted to be an athlete, but I was too puny. Like most kids, I dreamed of becoming a professional ball player. I played basketball, went out for football, ran track and played baseball. I was too small and slow. I had other friends who were small but extremely quick or jumped very high, etc. I had no such abilities. This really vexed me as I grew up. I figured if I could play sports it would help me to get to my goal of being rich. Which would allow me to be a secret Santa.

Day by day and year in, year out, I would pray to grow. I have tall family members. My prayers weren't answered. I prayed to grow taller. I ate so called growth foods. I would stretch myself because I heard that would help me to grow; all to no avail. I was little. I had the heart and will, but not the physical size. I had friends with the size but not the heart. I always thought God dealt me a short hand (no pun intended). I knew He was there, so why didn't He answer me? He not only didn't answer my growth prayers, but many other prayers in my life as well. I suppose a lot of people have these concerns, but mine seemed monumental at the time. I know now that I was off focus in life. Hindsight is so much better.

yes dem stairs got tacks on em,

and what they is givin' --I don't want em'

but I keeps worrying bout what I don't see,

but weez gone git thru it…won't we?

Well I knows God hears-He's got God sized ears

Maybe ize gone git there,--- one of deez years

My life became a quest for answers from God. Not that I ever doubted God was there. I knew He Is and Was always here. I believe most people have these questions. I didn't receive any satisfactory answers in church either. In fact, as time went on, I would become more and more dissatisfied with the whole organized religion thing. I saw how church leaders seemed to be powerless to live the kind of lives I heard them preach about. Most were worse than the non-churched in the world.

In 1965, Donn Pearce published the book **Cool Hand Luke**. Later, the movie was made with Paul Newman in the title role. On the surface, the movie is about life in a crude Florida prison. The movie is a cult classic. It has many memorable parts; the most famous being the line "what we have here, is failure to communicate". The real theme running throughout the screenplay however is Lukes' relationship with God. He wants answers from God, but is not getting them (to his satisfaction anyway). He even challenges God to strike him down during a storm to the horror of the other prisoners. Like Luke, I wanted a few answers from the Creator but answers were few and far between.

<u>REBELLION</u>

My rebellious stage started in my teens. I didn't so much rebel against society or my parents as much as I rebelled against the church. I still believed in God. I believed in Jesus Christ. I got caught up in looking at other people and their lives. Now that I'm an adult, I see it's a lot easier to be a punk, smart alec kid sitting back playing judge. I saw one local pastor who led a particularly poor Christian life openly. At least it wasn't to my standards.

Around the age of sixteen, I stopped willingly going to church. I say willingly because my mom and older sister would sometimes compel me to go. At one time, I decided I was going to consider being a Muslim. The Muslims seemed a lot more serious about their religion. Back then, you never heard about bombings and beheadings and the violence we see on the news these days. I never attended a meeting and I never read much in the Koran. What I did read wasn't setting too well with me. I swore off pork and inquired about changing my name to Amir. As soon as I swore off the swine, it seemed everyone, everywhere would be cooking and offering me yummy smelling pork chops and ribs. I stuck to my guns and abstained.

However, my faith in Islam weakened considerably after I read **The Autobiography of Malcolm X** in my senior year. He had apparently uncovered some hypocrisy with his mentors and leaders in the movement. He openly spoke out about his findings and he was openly murdered by them for his outspokenness. Great! Now where do I go? I continued to shun pork and grew into my young adult life.

Pontius Pilate asked *Jesus* "what is truth?" He didn't know Truth when he was staring Him in the face. I was the same way. I think most people are...

MY 1st NEAR DEATH EXPERIENCE

It happened when I was 20 yrs old. That would be thirty-three years ago, as I write this. I was in Kansas University Medical Center recovering from surgery, in a hospital bed. I had a chronically infected lymph gland near my throat that was removed. I'm allergic to **penicillin** so I was given a drug called **nafcillin** through an IV to combat post surgical infection.

As soon as I was hooked up to the IV, I started experiencing chest pains. I told the nurse. She told me it was normal and I had nothing to worry about. One nurse told me since the IV bag was cold, the medicine in it would cause pain at times as it entered my body. I pushed the nurse button several subsequent times and I was told I was okay. It's normal; I'm young and strong, etc. I was told it was no big deal by those attending nurses. This was the early afternoon.

GOD'S MESSAGE OF LOVE

Around 10:40 pm, as I lay in my hospital bed, hooked up to my IV, watching "**Nightline with Ted Koppel**", suddenly, I had a pain in my chest like a knife stabbing me with an elephant sitting on it. The worst pain I can remember. However, it only lasted a moment then I was immediately out of my body. I was looking down on my body lying on the bed. I could see the blue rays from the TV on my body. I could see and hear Ted Koppel still talking. I said to myself *what in the world is going on? Am I imagining this* I thought? Have I lost it? Am I dead? I knew I wasn't imagining this because I was more aware of everything than ever before. My senses seemed to be heightened. In fact, it seemed I knew what Ted Koppel was thinking. I really liked him before that experience; not so much afterwards.

I said, "God help me!"

Immediately, I was back in my body. I pushed the nurse button and my Dr. walked in. Dr. Hignight was his name. He had performed the operation. He wasn't usually there that time of night but happened to be coincidently. I told him what happened, including the out of body experience. He asked me if I had informed the nurses about my chest pains. I told him I'd told them several times. He believed me and yelled for the nurses to remove that "blankety blank" IV from my arm immediately.

After the IV was removed and the nurses had gone out of the room, he stepped back in and asked me about my experience again. He also believed me about my near-death experience. We didn't use the expression "Near Death Experience", I wouldn't hear that for another 30 years. He said he had been reading about this phenomenon. This changed my life in that I was a normal 20-year-old, thinking about girls and partying and other foolishness. I had also been wondering whether the Bible was true and if it contained the Truth. There is always some one around or in the media who is supposedly educated who tries to cast doubt on the veracity of God's Word.

As I mentioned earlier, I was talking about becoming a Muslim. I hadn't eaten pork in 3 yrs. Not one yummy pork chop or crispy slice of bacon. When I asked God for help, I knew Who answered my prayer. I don't know how I can explain it, but The God of my youth heard me; The God of church and Sunday school. He was still holding me. I knew from that moment on, that the God of the Bible Is God. When I got home from the hospital, I cooked me some bacon wrapped bacon.

LESSONS LEARNED

The first lesson I learned from this experience is that God Is definitely real. I also knew it was the God of the Bible. He Is the God of Abraham, Isaac and Jacob. He is also The God of Jesus Christ our Lord. Like I said, I don't how I knew it, but I knew it. He was familiar. He didn't say anything, but He let Himself be known. That part I've never doubted since.

The second lesson was "to be absent from the body is to be present with the Lord." Even though I didn't see Him, I knew He was there. I knew Who answered my prayer of desperation when I cried out "God save me". I was immediately in His presence. I was instantly in another realm. Most religious people I know don't know anything about this. Most I know don't believe it even though they hear about it in their services and sing songs about it. Some attribute it to the devil. I really don't care so much about their opinions, for I know what I saw and Who heard me and brought me back.

I wouldn't hear the term NDE or Near Death Experience for another 30 years. I was searching the internet for episodes of the television show *"I Survived, Beyond and Back"* when I stumbled upon the experiences of others. Many people have had difficulties in sharing their stories with others. They have told their doctors, pastors, priests, friends and family members etc., who have discouraged them, ridiculed them, humiliated them, rebuked them, told them they were crazy, they told them they were lying and so on. Some were even placed in psychiatric facilities. A lot of folks are afraid to tell their family members for fear of just these very things. I didn't need anyone else's opinion. I had always believed in a personal God. When I read about how others were treated when they told their stories, I thank Him for giving me strength. I didn't care one bit what others thought then or what they think now.

I don't know if the suicidal thoughts started then or not. All I know is, I had tasted eternity, and it didn't taste that bad. Since then I've studied near-death experience and found if they are not properly analyzed, discussed or interpreted with understanding people, the experiencer becomes depressed and/or suicidal. I was already depressed from the start.

I also lost all fear of death after this experience. As a matter of fact, I wanted to go. I knew there was something else besides this depressing world. I was more anxious than ever to get to it. When I first beheld suicide, she appeared plain and even frumpy to me, she was almost indistinguishable from the others. However, as we both matured, she became more and more attractive.

These stairs sho is slippery but I don't need no help

...keep yo pinions in yo head –hear what I said

... I can do this myself

ORLANDO

I was 20 years old when I had my first near death experience. I dropped out of college and was going nowhere fast when my sister Louise told me her job was transferring her from Chicago to Orlando. I hopped on a train to Chicago and moved to Central Florida with my sister, brother in law, niece and nephew. My brother in law Kevin is a lawyer and my sister Louise an insurance executive. Both graduated from Northwestern University in Evanston, Illinois where they met.

I was still battling my demons of depression. I had recently broken up with my girlfriend who had gone off to Iowa for college. Or should I say dumped by my girlfriend? That girlfriend would later become my first wife.

In the meantime, I enrolled in Hotel/Motel Management School at a local technical college in Orlando. I worked two jobs, full-time at a hotel and part-time at Pizza Hut at night. I was also in school full time. That part-time job at Pizza Hut would be instrumental in my second supernatural experience. I felt I didn't need much sleep.

I have always been a reader of autobiographies and biographies of successful people. I had read a biography of **Winston Churchill**. In that book, it said he took short catnaps throughout the day. He didn't sleep for long periods. For about a year, I did the same thing. I worked those two jobs and went to school. I belonged to a twenty-four-hour gym and any free time I had, I worked out. I would work on my physique. My goal was to be rich by age twenty- seven. I was still pursuing my goal of being a Secret Santa. That has always been my dream.

All that working and school with no sleep did take its toll me however. One night after working an extremely long week, I remember looking at my check stub. I had worked eighty-eight point nine hours in one week on just my hotel job. I had done this for many weeks in a row. I was trying to save up money to invest in real estate. I was extremely tired. I was exhausted in every way a person can be; physically, mentally, socially, emotionally and even spiritually, as I would soon find out.

One night, I got off work and headed home, I was staying in a house with a roommate at the time in Orlando. I sat down on the couch and turned on the television. As I did so, thought to myself *I'm sick and tired of being sick and tired.* I was at home alone. The show **The 700 Club** was on. I didn't want to watch it so I tried to change channels but the remote wouldn't work. I slapped the remote against my hand a few times, still getting nothing. I knew it wasn't the batteries because I'd just changed them before I went to work that day.

Right then, the show host. Ben Kinchlow said "there's a young man watching who is sick and tired of being sick and tired…"

Well that got even my stubborn attention to say the least. I'd just thought those exact words. What was he, a mind reader? *It must be God*, I reasoned, so I listened. Again, I want to say, I always believed in God. I believed in Jesus The Christ. I just had so many problems with churches.

To make a long story short, I prayed with the guy on *The 700 Club* to rededicate my life to The Lord. It was June 1985. I would need every ounce of that faith about a week later…

HELP! I'VE BEEN ROBBED!

About a week later, I was working my night job at Pizza Hut. The night seemed as normal as any other night. I was in Orlando, Florida at one of the Pizza Huts on Highway 50 or Colonial Drive. We had closed the store around 11 PM and I was cleaning up the back-kitchen area because I was the cook that night. I was also helping my friend Donna (who was a waitress that night) get her work finished so she could get home. Paul was the 6'8" hilarious Shift Leader for the night. Kerry was another waiter who worked on silverware. Kerry and Paul were excited about going to the Parliament House, an enormous dance club on Hwy 441 aka Orange Blossom Trail after work. Mary and another day waitress were in the lobby waiting for Paul and Kerry so they could go out and dance. I finished up first and left. I was going home. Kerry locked the door behind me and we said goodnight.

I walked out behind the building to my car, seeing two guys standing a few feet away near the dumpster. I was startled but I kept walking. One of the men was blond, the other had dark hair. I thought they were two young guys who worked the day shift in the same restaurant. They were facing away from me with their hands in their pockets. They both turned to face me and were wearing Halloween masks. Oh boy! Super oh boy! I continued to walk to my car and they walked along beside me. Great! This was getting better and better. They both had their hands in their pockets and didn't say a word.

They followed me to my car and stood on a small hill in front of me. Not a word was spoken; not by them anyway. I, on the other hand, was speaking in tongues of men or angels. I was allowed by them to get into my car and I started it. The suspicious guys were still standing on the hill as I drove off. I was parked behind the store so I pulled around front. Just then I saw Donna (our waitress) come out of the store so I stopped until she got in her car. I had the intent of going back in to the restaurant to tell Paul and Kerry to be careful, something fishy was going on out back.

Remember this was 1985 and there were no cell phones. As I got out of my car to go in to the restaurant, I saw a quick movement near Donnas' car from the corner of my eye and I started toward her without thinking. One of the masked hoodlums had pulled my sweet friend from her car and was holding a pistol to her head. They were at the rear left corner of the building; I was near the front on the same side. The other robber stood from behind her car and aimed a big, cannon like handgun at me.

"Come on hero!" he yelled. I put my hands up and stopped. "Put your F..ing hands down!' he yelled. I said "that's what they do on TV…" I still can't believe I said this out loud. They both laughed and said "we're going back in and having a party…" *Great!* I thought. I could've been gone home. But NO! Super dude here had to play good Samaritan.

As we were headed toward the front entrance, the words, "yea though I walk through the valley of the shadow of death, I will fear no evil" came to my mind. I became unusually calm. I can't explain the supernatural confidence I had. The malefactors had Donna and I go up to the door while they hid right next to us behind a trash can. From inside the restaurant, Kerry saw only Donna and I so he skipped over to the door to let us in. I tried to cut my eyes to let him know something was amiss but he didn't pay any attention and threw open the door.

"Donna and Victor are back!" Kerry said excitedly. Just then the robbers jumped up and stuck the gun in his face and yelled "party time!"

We were taken into the restaurant, placed on the floor with our faces down and hands behind our heads. One of the robbers shot the bomb sounding pistol when Paul continued to yell at and lecture them. They took us to the men's restroom and handcuffed half of us to the metal rail on the wall and the other half to the metal rail on the stall partition. Mary and the other day waitress hid under the booth in the lobby and were undetected by the crooks. They gave us instructions to stay there and not move. We kicked the bathroom partition down and those of us who were handcuffed to it went out and called the police after the robbers left. Poor

Kerry never recovered from this incident. He had a nervous breakdown and was taken away by ambulance. I never saw him again.

DO YOU CARE?

2 Cor. 12:2 and 12:3- *I know a man in Christ who fourteen years ago-- whether in the body I do not know, or out of the body I do not know, God knows-- such a man was caught up to the third heaven. 3.And I know how such a man-- whether in the body or apart from the body I do not know, God knows--4.was caught up into Paradise and heard inexpressible words, which a man is not permitted to speak..*

After all the police reports were done from the robbery and after the fire department cut off the handcuffs to free us, we were permitted to leave for our homes. It was around six o'clock in the morning. I was tired, drained and still shocked about the whole situation. On the way home, I ran over an armadillo and busted my radiator. My car had to be towed. My roommate picked me up and took me home. As I was finally about to lie down to sleep, I said a word of prayer. A prayer that would change my life forever.

"Lord, I thank You that we all got out of this horrible event safely. However Lord, there are people around the world who were in similar or worse situations who didn't make it. There were more robberies, burglaries, rapes, murders etc. Lord, You have all power, you could stop this…do YOU care?"

When I said the word care, I was taken up over the earth in the air. I could see the earth spinning very fast. On the earth, I started to see tragic scenes, images, real scenes. I saw a baby starving to death, I saw a woman being attacked. I saw images of devastation and famine. With every separate image, I felt a physical pain in my heart. The pain was so much beyond any pain a human can possibly feel. It was indescribable. The best I can compare it to is if you swallowed a nuclear bomb and it exploded inside of you. I felt this ultra intense physical, emotional, spiritual pain with every image, every scene. Then God spoke to me and said…

"This is how I hurt when people hurt; don't ever ask me if I care again…"

I was immediately back in my bedroom. I had been awake almost 24 hours. I hadn't been able to get to sleep when I got home or get my regular naps because of the robbery. After this happened, I couldn't sleep if I tried.

To say I was amazed is an understatement. I was humbled. I was ashamed that I'd asked such a thing. I didn't understand how everything works in this world, but I knew *and* know without a shadow of a doubt that God cares. And I know one person who'll never ask that question of God again. I wish He'd answer prayers quickly every time. Maybe not so dramatically but promptly. Maybe I'll find out in Heaven why He chose to answer at all. I suppose He wanted me to know He really does care.

I don't know why God does things the way He does. If I were Him, I'd do things differently. In the Bible, when John the Baptist was in prison and would soon be executed, he sent his followers to Jesus to ask if Jesus was the promised one or should they wait for another. John was in a desperate situation and thought God would probably deliver him from his crisis. Maybe he thought what I thought; "if You have all power, do something!" Jesus answered with a demonstration of healing miracles along with other miracles. He sent John's disciples to him and said "tell John how the sick are healed and the dead are raised. Then Jesus said "blessed are those who are not offended because of me." He does things His own way. It never seems to be the way we expect Him to do it. His ways are not our ways. He didn't answer me in the way I thought He would. A simple yes would have sufficed, but He showed me and allowed me to feel His pain. What a mighty God we serve!

Something else happened to me in that experience also. I was given an empathy, I guess you can say, for people. Now when someone is in close proximity to me, I can feel the emotions they are feeling. It took me many years to figure this out. I'm still in the learning stages.

Spiritual things are talked about in some churches, but they weren't taught where I attended services. Most church people are ignorant and afraid of the spirit world. Nowadays I have a better understanding and I have accepted this as a gift from God. If someone is sad, I can't be happy next to them. I've cried for people I don't even know and couldn't stop. I thought I was going crazy for years until I began to understand this gift and from whence it came. I feel the love from others, hate, bitterness, rejection, sadness, sorrow, joy or whatever they are feeling in that moment.

Most of the time I'm a loner so I won't get drained with someone else's emotions on top of my own. This came out of my experience of being taken up by God and allowed to see things the way He sees them. I didn't understand for many years why my emotions would be all over the place. It took me nearly 30 years to figure out what happened to me after reading about a lady who had a similar experience.

LESSONS LEARNED

The number one lesson I learned from that experience is that God is there. We may not always perceive Him. I may not have always heard His voice correctly or at all; but He Is there. Jehovah-Shammah.

The second thing is God cares. He cared enough to show a cook at Pizza Hut that He cares.

Thirdly, God feels our pain and joy. When we experience joy and pain or any other emotion, especially the emotion of love, He feels it for God Is Love.

1 John 4:7-9

7Beloved, let us love one another, for love is from God; and everyone who loves is born of God and knows God. 8The one who does not love does not know God, for God is love. 9By this the love of God was manifested in us, that God has sent His only begotten Son into the world so that we might live through Him...

Number four is if you have an encounter with God, you'll never be the same. The fifth lesson is God is merciful! He could've smacked me around, but He allowed me to see a greater picture than I could ever imagine. And lastly, don't ask Him if He cares…whew!

After this I really wanted to know more about God so I started reading the Bible all the way through. I started in 1985 and I still do it now. Each time I read it through, it's brand new. The Word is alive. Each time I read it, I see things I would've sworn weren't there the previous time. Each time, I see the verses in a new light, though they never change. It seemed, the more I read, the more introspective I became.

I was learning more and more, but my depression never lifted. In fact, it seemed to get worse. I did what most people do when they first read the Bible. I became more smug, more religious.

GOD'S MESSAGE OF LOVE

He looked into the Word, things grew clearer and clearer,

in fact them crystal stairs started to resemble a mirror;

but it seemed I was further away rather than drawing nearer..

In June of 1985, I left Orlando and moved back to Kansas City. After my second experience, my priorities changed. I no longer cared to be rich. I still wanted to serve and give, but I wasn't sure how I was supposed to go about it. Who would I serve? What did I have to give? I didn't have any money to give, that's for sure. The priority, I thought, should be home so I concentrated on helping my mother around the house. My older brother, whom I love dearly, had been diagnosed with schizophrenia also. He was living at home with my mom. I could keep him company and give her a little more peace of mind.

I joined a large, active church in Kansas City, Missouri. I started out in Help Ministries. I would help in any way I could. I would clean, cut grass, worked in the nursery, prayer team. I cooked for any event, set up chairs, painted, worked with disrespectful teens, you name it. If they needed help I could offer, I was there.

I wiped hundreds of tiny noses, changed diapers, watched Veggie Tales over and over, rocked babies to sleep and loved every minute of it. I was serving in the best ways I could. I was doing all of that, still reading my Bible through and taking ministry courses. I read the Bible from cover to cover because I'd heard preachers attribute quotes and sayings to the Word that just weren't there. I wanted to know for myself. I knew several of the associate pastors very well.

WHAT'S LOVE GOT TO DO WITH IT?

One day while driving home from work, I thought I saw my ex- girlfriend in my rear-view mirror. She was the same ex-girlfriend that went away to college and broke up with me. It looked like she was following me so I pulled over but she kept going. The very next day there was a letter from her in my mailbox; her dad worked for the post office. She kind of apologized for dumping me and asked if I would talk to her again. We started dating again and got married the same year. I was 25 years old when I first married. My wife and I both got involved in the church. She sang on our church television program. She helped in the nursery also. We took care of the two and three-year olds. As far as I could see, we were getting along pretty well. As far as I could see anyway.

Two years later we had a daughter. We named her after me, Victoria or Tori. When I first saw her, I was so amazed I couldn't speak. I couldn't take my eyes off her. She was absolutely the most beautiful thing I'd ever laid eyes on! She still is. She is twenty-six years old and every time I see her, it's still like the first time. We later had two sons, Victor and Aaric, both beautiful young men. My love for them is the same.

I loved being a dad. I'd prayed for a wife and children since I was a child. I put together a fun school classroom in our house for the kids. I had "*Hooked on Phonics and The Phonics Game*". I had maps, charts, alphabets, chalkboards and an abacus. We went on field trips. I read them stories and encouraged them to create their own. Now things were looking up. I was saving up every dime I could because I wanted to start buying and flipping properties. My wife also saved money for our goals. I was riding higher than a flea on a giraffes' forehead. Things were going well. Life was great! Then…

KA POW!

I worked nights, keeping the children in the day. My wife worked days and kept them at night. One day I came home from work like any other, I was probably whistling as I came to the door. My kids were usually there to meet me and we would wrestle on the living room floor as soon as I walked in. My youngest son Aaric was two years old.

When I got to the door, I put my key in the lock but it didn't work. I tried again and again. I stepped back and looked to see if I was at the right address. I was. I started knocking on the door. I could hear my children inside but no one came to the door. What in the world was going on?

Well, my wife had taken up with another man and changed the locks on the door. I had no idea. I knew she was a little more distant than usual but I had been praying about that and working on myself. My mother had told me a couple of years before that this would happen but I didn't want to hear that. She had a guy that she worked with on her job and immediately filed for divorce. I tried to talk to her but she wouldn't talk to me. To say I was shocked, is an understatement for sure. I had a whole gamut of emotions going on as one would guess. I was confused, betrayed, angry, sad, ashamed, and humiliated.

She had already told the staff at church. I called the pastor in charge of marriage counseling and he told me he didn't want to talk to me. The same guy I had worked with, prayed with and worshiped with for years told me he wouldn't talk to me. I was livid to say the least. If I had seen him, I would've broken his neck. I went to live at my mothers' house in the basement.

One day during this ordeal, I turned on my church television show and saw my pastor. He went on to say concerning me," I don't know how a man can just walk out on his wife and three little children…" I was so devastated, deserted, dumbfounded and distraught I didn't know what to do. I never went back to that church again. To top it off, I had been laid off my job recently, and was working a security gig. I was making six bucks an hour in the middle nineties and my child support was assessed at $585 a month. You add the taxes taken from my check, which would leave roughly 30 dollars every two weeks on my paychecks. How was that even legal? In Wyandotte County, Kansas, it was legal. I had it going on.

> *Yo fortunes and dreams is plunging and plunging-*
>
> *who knew deez crystal stairs lead to the dungeon?*
>
> *Looks like deez wells of yours done run dry-*
>
> *He's got arrows, youz the bullseye---*
>
> *eli eli lama sabathani*

I had lost my wife, my children, my home, my job, my church, my dreams for my family life, my family (for I loved my in-laws) and my health also took a dive, allegedly from the stress of the whole ordeal. I also lost things you can't see like self esteem, confidence, sense of well being, hope for the future and at times I thought I was losing my mind. I prayed but found no answers like in **Cool Hand Luke**. My God, my God why hast thou forsaken me?

I turned my anger towards Heaven. How could He allow this to happen? Was I not serving Him? Was I not being a good husband and father? Apparently not! I continued to live in my mothers' basement. I hate spiders but there was one near the couch I slept on that I became fond of. I was losing my grip. I kept working and tried to keep up a front of having it together. One day my niece (who is tough) walked in the house and took one look at me and burst into tears. I guess I looked just that pitiful.

I had to find someone to blame so after God, I blamed myself. That was short lived because at the suggestion of my sister, who swore I must have done something to cause this catastrophe, I asked my wife. I knew my sister was wrong but I asked her anyway. I wanted to make sure. She told me to my face "it's nothing you've done. This is something I wanted to do…" Well, what can you say to that?

She became colder than a well-diggers belt buckle towards me. Meanwhile, my faith in everything good became as weak as diluted water. This situation most certainly gave me empathy for people going through similar circumstances. I would have rather never been born than have gone through this. It was a pain that seemed to never end. I missed my kids especially. We were very close. Now if I saw them at all, it was every other Tuesday. I was working so much to keep up on my child support that I couldn't take a weekend off. If you missed a child support payment in Wyandotte County, Kansas, you went straight to jail. I was not trying to do any time behind bars.

I was back to blaming God. After all, He'd protected Sarah and rebuked two different kings for Abraham. He did it even though Abraham gave his wife away to save his own skin. Why couldn't He fight for me? Was I not serving Him? Was I not serving Him in the right spirit? I was back to blaming myself. I was on a perpetual ride on the emotional roller coaster. I didn't know how to get off. My near and dear companion depression was there with me, big time. Like I said before, at first suicide looked plain and unattractive to me, however as she grew older, her curves got my attention more and more.

Hello darkness my ol' friend,

fancy seeing you here again..

can't says that I missed you;

it's hard to hide behind stairs of crystal

and despair, he's here with you

There is a scripture that says God hates divorce. I know why now, it's a horrible thing. There really are no resources for men going through divorce. I talked to an employee assistance counselor once who told everyone on my job what we talked about. The church was the worst place to go. Maybe because I expected too much as far as understanding and compassion. I found neither. I was rebuked, ridiculed, shunned, and told to "man up". Told if I hadn't done "this or that" and on and on. I heard a lot of Christianese and religious jargon. I wasn't trying to shirk my duties as a husband or father. I did not run out on my family. I was told I had done both.

I thank God for a couple from my church named Joe and Wendy Chavez. They took me in to their family and showed me love. They didn't even know me. They invited me over to eat, prayed for me, encouraged me and just all around showed me love. It's their compassion that allowed me to make it through this horrible time in my life. God bless them for their kindness.

The only people I could talk to were my mother and my oldest sister. Thankfully, they were enough to keep me going one day at a time.

Also during this time, I lost my father, who passed away in 1997. I was laid off my job around the same time. I also ended up in the Telemetry Unit at Bethany Medical Center for a "stress related" heart incident. The good times were rolling in my life for sure. I was taking more of a beating than Rhonda Rousey's sparring partner and the blood letting had just begun.

De Ja Vu –All Over Again

I moved on with my life still in anguish. I muddled through somehow. In 1998, I began my career as a deputy sheriff. I worked my way up to the rank of sergeant. I was a **SWAT** Team Assistant Team Leader. My career was doing okay even though my home life was horrible. Elijah, a friend of mine, asked me to go one night to play pool. I hadn't gone anywhere except work in a long while so I went. That night I met a lady who would become a lifelong friend.

One day she invited me to meet her other new friend who was a pastor. I'd had it up to there with pastors but she kept bothering me so I went. He was a great guy. He also became a lifelong friend. We went to his church on Easter Sunday 1999. While I was there, I met a woman whom I thought tried too hard to be noticed. I didn't say much to her that day but continued to go to that church every so often and even joined later. To make a long story short, me and this woman started dating and were married on Christmas day 1999.

In retrospect, I believe she should have remained a great friend also but NOOOOOOOOOO. I had to go and mess up a perfectly good friendship. A month or so into the marriage she moved away for a few days; then came back. This pattern would repeat over the years with different excuses.

In 2005, I left the sheriff department full time and remained on as a reserve officer. I went to work for a US Marshal contract inmate holding facility in Leavenworth, Kansas where I rose to the rank of Captain.

I worked in my church as a teacher. I taught the adult Bible class, the teenage class and preached some Sunday mornings when the pastor was away. I was an avid Bible reader and studier. I read the Bible through several more times. I took several more Bible courses. I did my best to show the love I thought church people were supposed to show.

In 2007, my 2nd wife filed for divorce. Several years after the divorce, she told why she would leave again and again. She was stuck on one of her college instructors and every time she thought she might have a chance to get in, she would leave. During the marriage, I was confused. I was wondering what I was doing wrong. Now I know what I was doing wrong-- getting married. I felt lower than a snake's belly under a wagon wheel. My new motto became "love is a four-letter word, like crap".

Not long before the time of the divorce proceedings, my mom passed away. On top of that, my soon to be ex-wife started dating one of my coworkers and they delighted in "rubbing it in my face" like acne crème. Of course I blamed myself first, then God for not killing me before I got into that predicament. I had believed if you did your best in a marriage maybe God would somehow pick up the slack. I figured I wasn't supposed to be married maybe. One mess yes, two you're through.

If one more person had said to me "God won't give you more than you can handle" or "God has something better for you" or so on…I'd be writing this from a prison cell now. If a person who is going through hell doesn't ask for your advice, shut up! Pray for them if you just must say something. I was so sick of well meaning folk giving me their stupid opinions. I had it up to there with them telling me what I should have done or not done!

Most of time, I was thinking I shouldn't have been born at all. How does that work? Good ol' church people were the last folks I looked forward to seeing. I got more compassion from a rock than most of them. I honestly received more help from strangers. I believe the reason I went through some of those things was so I could become a more compassionate person.

In the book of Job, he lost his children to tragedy, lost his home, lost his wealth, lost his status in the community and his wife turned on him. Job blamed God. Then along comes his religious friends to tell him how sinful he must have been for God to do all of this to him. They were taking up for God. They had the Almighty all figured out. Job maintained his integrity. In the end, God showed up and showed Job His Glory. He also added a lesson or two in humility. However, God loved Job and restored him double for the trouble he had endured, but God had less patience with his friends. He rebuked them and told them they should have been more compassionate, merciful and sympathetic. God also told them He was going to tell Job to pray for them. He told them if Job didn't pray for them, they'd be sorry.

Few things burn my bloomers more than Job's comforters, the people who tell you what you did or shouldn't have done while you're going through trauma or painful situations. Later, you see those same big mouth pseudo friends folding like origami when they face their own trials.

On top of all that, I had a fifty thousand dollar plus income tax bill which I incurred because of bankruptcy. I couldn't pay that in 50,000 years on my salary. My teenage son had come to live with me, but left to live with a friend of his. I was in the middle of a rift with my family over the house we grew up in and my blood pressure was routinely running in the low 200s over 140 something. I still had gigantic child support payments coming out of my checks along with humongous doctor bills. Suicide appeared to me as a bombshell now, in heels and skimpy clothes. Va Va voom!

When it rains; it poze-

'specially on dem stairs of yoze…

careful nah, don't you fall…

theyz being so slippery and all

maybe yuze listening to too many voices

maybe it's yo stupid choices

I knew God had forsaken me. I was in depression overload. I suppose most people would be under the circumstances. I just didn't know how to get the answers I needed. I went to see a counselor with the insurance plan on my job. He said if he'd been going through what I was, he'd lose his mind. He told me I was strong. Yeah right. In my mind, I was going down faster than a peregrine falcon diving on prey. Something had to give.

Indeed, something had to give. Like everyone else, I had to keep living. Like others, I had to live day to day with inner heartache and pain. Like others, I put on a good face and showed up. I still did my best to be an encouragement to others. Most of my coworkers were going through family related suicides, **PTSD**, divorce, cancer, etc. We were a bunch of hurting souls helping one another. I thank God for those wonderful people at the **Leavenworth Detention Center**.

I even started dating a girl from work. We worked different shifts so I rarely saw her. She'd asked me out first so we became friends or at least I thought we were friends. In retrospect, I shouldn't have been seeing anyone in a romantic sense. I lived alone at that time, in a one-bedroom apartment.

Is He hearin' me?

He won't relent

GOD'S MESSAGE OF LOVE

His face is against me

Hard like a flint

He's not a man that He should repent

Dun worked all deez years and come to nuthin'

lot easier to go down stairs,

Than to come up 'em

PART 2

The date was April 27th, 2010. It seemed to be a typical day for me. It was a sunny day but very cold. I had reached the rank of Captain in my profession. A regular shift for me at this period in my life consisted of 12 to 16-hour days, six days a week. Some days lasted 20 hours or more. I worked the day shift, allegedly. The scheduled hours were from 6 am to 6 pm; however, things hardly ever went as scheduled. I remember one night when I was so exhausted near the end of my shift, I could barely move.

Right at the end of our final count, I was called over the radio. The call came from a very good and capable officer, Rebecca, who rarely called for supervisors so I knew something was wrong. The call was for me to come to her area ASAP. I bolted from my office and when I arrived at the area known as Q building, I saw an inmate there hardly recognizable as a human. He had been beat up by members of his own Hispanic gang. I believe he was left to die. He was conscious and refusing medical attention.

He was stating that he was a "G"; whatever G stood for, maybe Goner in this case. Anyway, he was shipped to the emergency room immediately.

This incident and the subsequent reports took several more hours of work. The first of those hours are run on adrenaline. When that adrenaline runs out, it's not good. Sometimes I would be so tired, I didn't remember the trip home.

Mr. "G" survived that trauma by the way, and thanked us later for saving his life. He had a broken clavicle, several broken ribs, one arm broken in two places, the other arm was broken also, a concussion and several facial fractures; various cuts, bumps and contusions, but he lived. These kinds of events would happen regularly. They always tended to happen near the end of the shift.

Each day I supervised around 30 to 35 officers per shift, about 15 medical staff, 10 or so inmate case counselors, the maintenance department and over 1100 inmates at a Correctional facility in Leavenworth, Kansas. I also worked as a reserve deputy sheriff at the Wyandotte County Sheriff Department in my home city of Kansas City, Kansas.

I lived alone at that period in my life. I've lived alone about ninety percent of my adult life, even when I was married. My eldest son was a young teenager and had been living with me. He had gotten angry over the whole "get up and go to school" thing and moved out of my place to live with a friend of his. I had just broken up with my girlfriend who had been my friend for about a year. We worked opposite shifts so we never saw each other anyway. It still felt like I was losing again. I was still broke financially. Child support took three quarters of my salary; taxes took the rest. I owed the IRS over 50 thousand dollars. I also owed the state of Kansas over 11 thousand dollars. If I lived as long as Methuselah lived, I would've never been able to pay off those debts on my salary. This caused me so much anguish and stress, I had medical bills also. I couldn't afford to take a day off to spend with my kids because it would throw me even further behind in my bills. I was still missing my children every day. I felt like the biggest failure in the annals of human history.

My relationship with my siblings was strained over a real estate dispute. I cursed the day I was born whenever I thought of my ex-wives. Moreover, I was physically and emotionally drained. The top number for my blood pressure had been in the 200s all that week. I refused to see another doctor and rack up another huge medical bill. I was tired, very tired. Tired of losing everything I loved and held dear, tired of being without money, tired of feeling there was no hope for anything to change for the better. I was just plain tired of life. It seemed like no good news ever came, only one train after another came through the tunnel. Every one of them had a light in the front appearing to bring hope, yet, every one of them seemed to run me over.

This day, however, would be different. This day would be eternally different. Like I said, it started out like any other day. I went to work as I normally did. I remember my boss (the warden) being in a particularly good mood. My head was pounding from a high blood pressure headache. I had been going back and forth in an argument with my ex-girlfriend through email. I remember my partner at work and sweet friend (my lieutenant) Pattie feeling my pain. She feels the pain of others. God sent her as my wonderful friend and sister. She was the first person who found out from me what happened that day.

> *They sayz God cares, so Ize says my prayers,*
>
> *But if that's so, why'd I fall down these crystal stairs,*
>
> *Been dealing with the bumps and bruises,*
>
> *Not so well with the glares*

Like I said, the day started off like any other day. I was sitting in my office at around 2 pm. I had been asking God for some time to take me out of here. I had at least given Him my expressed written consent. My ex-girlfriend was in an emailing mood that day. I didn't have the patience for her foolishness or anyone else's for that matter. My head was throbbing from a blood pressure headache. I had decided that nothing was ever going to work out. My whole life was beat up from the feet up and I was fed up. So, I got up and walked out of work. I didn't care if I lost my job or whatever. I jumped in my truck and went straight home. I was in anguish like George Bailey on *"It's a Wonderful Life"* when Uncle Billy lost the bank deposit.

A NEW DAY

When I arrived home, I laid down on my bed. Like I said, I was living alone in a small one-bedroom apartment in Leavenworth Kansas. I decided I'd enough of life so I wanted to end it. As I was lying there, I heard a voice say, "don't shoot yourself…you don't want your son to find you like that."

I thought that was absurd because I hadn't seen or talked to my son in weeks. He had moved out and was living with his friends. Anyway, I heeded the voice and remembered I had just bought a big bottle of Benadryl from the surplus store. It contained 500 pills. I had been raised a Christian but I didn't know if I killed myself what would happen to my soul.

I was so tired of life at that time, I didn't care; I just wanted to die. I got the bottle of medicine and began to take them. It took me 4 or 5 big gulps but I took them all and laid back down on my bed. I felt a sense relief and a dread all at the same time. I felt relief that this journey of disappointment and pain would finally be over. I felt fear because I wasn't sure if God would be pleased with my decision.

Anyway, the deed was done. I could start to feel the drug taking effect on my body. I became extremely thirsty. Parts of my body started becoming numb. Then I heard the front door open.

"Dad!" I heard. It was my son. I couldn't answer him back. "Dad?" As he walked into my bedroom.

"Water…" I was all I could squeeze out.

"What's wrong?" He asked. I couldn't answer, I was too weak at this point. He ran to get me a glass of water but I couldn't drink it. I was drifting in and out of consciousness as I heard him call 911 for help.

When the EMTs arrived, I was nearly gone. I remember them asking what happened. They asked if I had taken anything. I shook my head no. I remember them saying they were going to a hospital that was far away, and I wondered about that. When I was placed in the ambulance, there was one technician in the back with me. He was not empathetic to me or my situation. He was being a smartass. Also, when he thought I was unconscious or dead, he wrenched my right arm very hard. I still have trouble with my right shoulder to this day.

I tried to take my mind off the situation and prayed that all would be well whether I lived or died. I had been silently praying the whole time. Sometime on the way to the hospital, I was no longer in the ambulance. My mind, body and soul checked out.

NO CONDEMNATION

When I left this realm, so to speak, I saw a Light. Not just any Light. **The Light! The Light of all lights. The Light of the world. GOD**.

Some people ask...how do you know? There's no satisfactory answer for that. When you're in God's presence, you know. He was brighter than ten thousand suns but it didn't hurt my eyes. I have heard others describe it similarly since my experience, but no amount of words can even come close to articulating it. The only thing I can liken it to is; it was like the first flash of a nuclear bomb. He is Pure Light with no darkness at all. I didn't see any human features or form; only Light, only Love. He Is Pure, Holy, unconditional Love. A love higher, deeper, wider and more expansive than anyone can describe. There really are no human words that even come close.

I was in eternity now. A temporal jargon can't begin to paint a picture of eternal. He was Light, but He was also Love at the same time. He knew me. He knew what I was thinking. He knew I was thinking I should be in hell since I had taken those pills.

He said, "I have no condemnation for you…"

When I say "He said" I mean He spoke, but not words as we normally speak. It was eternal speech…soul to soul. There was no visible mouth that I could see, but the words came to me. This phrase "no condemnation" confused me because it wasn't a phrase I even used.

Also, I wasn't aware that this was the root of my problems. I had been condemning myself all my life, while God hadn't been condemning me at all. Then He took me and placed me inside of the Love and Light. It was like I was being placed in a deep swimming pool. There were differences however. When you're in a pool, you are there in your body separate from the water, even though you're in the water. In my case, I was in this baptism of

Love but I became a part of that Love. I was one with the Light and the Love. It was kind of like an ice cube being thrown into a hot whirlpool. When I realized I was a part of Him, I knew instinctively that I was at Home and I didn't want to leave.

Then He said to me "your life is not yours to take..."

I then noticed I was standing there and the Light turned into liquid. It was a thick liquid like butter milk. He poured the Light into me from the top of my head and went down to the soles of my feet healing me as it went down my body. When the Light and Love hit the soles of my feet, I awoke in the emergency room at St. Luke's hospital in Kansas City, Missouri. I saw my ex-wife standing there talking to a physician, then my son Aaric.

I didn't remember, at the time, what had just happened to me. I knew something had happened but I couldn't remember what. I felt like I had been hollowed out and refilled. I was not happy about being back at first. I didn't know why. Nothing had changed in the natural. I still had bills on top of bills to pay. I still had no money to pay them. I had a miserable life in terms of relationships. The rest of my family soon came in to see me, including brothers and sisters, nieces and nephews and friends.

The time was around one in the morning. I had gone to the hospital at about 4 pm the day before. The doctor told my ex-wife I was okay to leave and I was taken home to Leavenworth by my children. We didn't talk about what happened on the way home. I was exhausted and went to bed. I thanked God for allowing me to get through my ordeal even though nothing external had seemingly changed. I had no recollection of my celestial experience until the next morning.

When I woke up the next morning, I remembered what happened. I remembered being loved. I remembered being in the Light. I remembered the words and compassion. I remembered I still had a lot of things on my plate but I knew it would be alright.

Made a mistake

Fuh goodness sake

GOD'S MESSAGE OF LOVE

Er'body know dat crystal is easy to break

Wait...

Is dat the end of dis tunnel I see?

Otta da night

Gotta be right

Please be right

Light shining thru dem glass stairs at me

Over the next week or so after my experience, it seemed everyone I knew came to see or called me. Every one of them had a story of something we had done or talked about before my incident. Apparently, I had touched more lives (for the good) than I had realized. Different people told me of how I'd encouraged them, gave them a hand, prayed with them, etc. So many talked about how I treated them honorably when they felt unworthy. Let that be a lesson for everyone reading this book. You are touching peoples' lives whether you know it or not. People are watching you. I thank God so many friends contacted me, remembering me doing good things.

So many people thanked and hugged me. Some people heard I had died. I don't know if I was declared dead by the physician, but I got the opportunity, privilege and blessing to see what I saw. I have worked on people who have been seemingly dead in my profession. One was a guy inside the jail who suffered a heart attack. Several nurses, other officers and emergency personnel and I performed CPR on him for over 25 minutes. He had no pulse, heartbeat, or breathing. He finally came back after being shocked with the paddles several times. I was sure he was a dead man.

The inmates in the facility where I worked heard I'd been found unresponsive and different groups, both male and female, said they had prayer services for me. The female inmates all signed a Get Well card for me. It was like I was living the last scene in the movie **It's A Wonderful Life**. The part when the whole town of Bedford Falls showed up to save good ole George Bailey from the bank examiners, except no one brought me money.

I felt better in the sense that at least I knew God had me here. I knew I must have an important purpose. I've since realized we all do. I used to say I believed that before my experience but I don't know how much I really was certain of it.

<u>LIFE GOES ON</u>

Shortly after my brush with eternity, I left the facility in Leavenworth and continued my career as a full-time deputy sheriff. I was ordained as a minister at a Non-Denominational Christian organization. I became a different person in that I can't hold grudges any more. I became friends with my second ex-wife. I hadn't spoken to her in over five years. She helped me find an accountant. That accountant negotiated with the Internal Revenue Service and reduced my tax bill to 4,500 dollars. My ex-wife helped pay it off.

As a matter of fact, both exes are friends of mine now. Life for me still ain't been no crystal stair; but it's a lot better knowing that God is with me. I know now that my life counts for something. Also, knowing I'm not under condemnation from God alleviates the stress of trying to perform for Him. He loves me (and you) anyway. If God be for me, who can be against me? That dark cloud of depression is a thing of the past. God doesn't take away your problems, He gives you a different perspective on them. I believe now that no struggle or situation (adverse or not) is wasted with God. He is making us fit for His Kingdom. In His Kingdom, the unlovable are loved. We as people must be taught that. I suppose that's an easier lesson for some to grasp than others. Maybe there are those who can get it by reading about it. I, unfortunately had to get it hands on.

Bumps an' bruises and all

Git up! Weez all fall

Stuff is happnin fuh a reason-

even trees look dead winter season

Sum times when yuze down is when they reach ya

Who knew tumbling down stairs was such a good teacha

Too bad I couldn't lernt from just hearin' the preacha

WHAT I LEARNED

I learned several things from my near-death experiences...

I learned that God loves us.

Sure, we read and talk about a kind of almost generic love of God. We have no earthly idea the kind of Love God has for us. There are and I repeat, there are no human words to describe the pure, unadulterated, unconditional, untainted, wonderful love He has for you and me.

I learned what I thought I already knew, that is, a person is "saved" for accepting God's free gift of life through Christ. You are accepted because of what Jesus did and Who He Is. We are never made children of God on our own merits. Never.

When I thought I should have deserved hell, my God spoke words of no condemnation. He didn't just tell me that He loved me, He placed me inside of Love. He baptized me in Love. Imagine that, a baptism in God's great love. That Love Is God Himself. I was never sure if one committed suicide, whether they'd be forgiven or not. I believed this was decided on a case by case basis. No two suicides are the same. No two situations are the same. No two people are the same. In my case, I was in grief and depression for years. I not only grieved for me, I had sorrow for the pain in others. God calls that love and compassion. God understood and had compassion on me. He understood the source of my sorrow when I didn't. He even told me before I did it not to shoot myself. If I had destroyed my body in such a way I wouldn't have been able to return and complete my mission here on earth. Oh, what a wonderful God we serve!

I can't speak for anyone else's suicide attempt or completion. He told me "my life is not mine to take…" At the time, I was thinking "well whosevers' life it is to take, please take it…" Now I see His great wisdom and mercy and compassion. I've been able to lead more people to the Lord effortlessly where it used to be a challenge to me. Now I just tell my story and that starts testimony time; supernatural testimony time. To Him be the Glory!

No, my life is not my own. That's actually liberating in the sense that we can know someone greater is looking out for us. We belong to Him. Hallelujah!

God also knew I wanted answers. Who am I? Why am I here? What am I supposed to do? Why is there so much suffering in the world? What's this whole "life" thing about? What are the winning Powerball numbers and so forth? In the Bible, Jesus answered questions with questions. At least 29 times in the New Testament He answered questions with a question. I had gone for years looking for answers and found out that He really Is the Answer. God deals with and reveals the real problems we face. He doesn't even answer (most times) the questions we thought were so important. Our Father answers the big question or questions. It's like knowing someone owes you 100 dollars, you're anticipating getting the 100 when the person gives you 100 thousand dollars. When I got to see and experience God's Light and Love; all of those other questions were more than answered. Except the Powerball numbers of course.

DOCTRINE

I understand that a lot of people in the NDE community don't believe in hell. I heard one say "I was saved as a little girl but I hadn't been living for God when I died. I was expecting judgment." There is no condemnation if you're in Christ. He took it for us on the cross. We're not sinners because we sin anyway. The Bible says we are all sinners because of Adams' sin. Consequently, those of us who trust in Jesus are righteous because of His righteousness. I don't know about you, but to me that's wonderful news. I don't have to worry about my deeds. Neither do you if we accept His gift of forgiveness. The Bible says that He is not willing for anyone to perish. He wants us to accept His gift of eternal life. He gave us free will. If we do perish it's because we are willing to rebel or ignore this gift. Please don't! there are no do overs in life.

- I learned without a shadow of a doubt that the God of the Bible is God.

- As I pen this book, Christianity is under tremendous attack in America. Most believers don't recognize it or are in denial. If there is not a drastic change in direction soon, Christ will be illegal here. Jesus said, "If they hated Me; they will hate you..." He also said, "this is the condemnation of the world, that Light came into the world and the world didn't receive Him because their deeds were evil..."

- We have been spoiled in the U. S. We often forget that being a follower of Christ means a death sentence in many countries. It's well on its way to meaning the same in the good ole US of A. Increasingly, Christ and His followers are painted and portrayed as villains, hatemongers, phobics and the like.

Like I said earlier, in my teens I'd had enough of playing church and I decided to be serious about religion. Little did I know, religion was the last thing I needed. So, I made up my mind I was going to find out what being a Muslim was all about. I stopped eating pork. I didn't eat even one slice of crispy, smoky bacon. I was going to change my name to Amir. My first near death experience (that I can remember anyway) put those ideas to rest. I knew who brought me back. There's no way to explain how you know, but you know. I knew it was the God I knew from a child. It was the God of the Bible. He Is God of all gods. He Is God the Father of Jesus Christ. He loves us all, Muslims included, and He has provided the Way to Him.

I learned that God knows me so well. Before my near-death experience in 2010, I had never read about these experiences. Since then, I've read many near death experiences because I saw a television show called *I Survived Beyond and Back* on cable. This got me really interested in other people's NDEs. I started looking them up on YouTube and other social media. I began to see just how prevalent this phenomenon is all over the world. Every one of them has similarities, yet everyone is unique.

GOD'S MESSAGE OF LOVE

A common theme in a lot of these journeys is when God will ask the person if they want to return to their bodies. Some return for their kids or spouses. Some return for completion of their personal missions.

God knew better than to ask me if I wanted to return. I believe that is why I didn't remember my adventure until the next day. If He had asked me if I wanted to go back He would've had to get Michael, Gabriel, Uriel and more angels to get me out of there. He knew full well I did not want to return. I don't want to sound suicidal because I'm not, but I'm ready to go again. This took away any fear I had of death. I say this carefully because I don't want to be misunderstood. I don't want my wife and children to think I don't want to be with them; I do. However, once you've tasted pure, unconditional love; the love of God Almighty, nothing else compares. There are no words spoken to articulate our Father's affection for us.

Jesus Is Real.

I've gotten flack from people saying that Jesus is someone that man made up to make us behave. You hear that a lot in black communities. I have relatives and so-called friends who have unfriended me on Facebook because of what I believe about Jesus. Adios! Don't let the "like" button hit you where the Good Lord split you. I don't know where this foolishness comes from. I don't care from whence it comes. I know Jesus Is Real. Jesus Is God.

- God hates religion.

- Religion is the opposite of true Christianity.

- Religion says you can earn or work your way to God. Christ says there is one way to the Father; through Him.

- Not our works-His sacrifice.

Religious people hated Jesus. They studied about God. They taught about God. They tried to act like they believed they should act, but when it came down to it, they didn't know God when they spit in His face.

Jesus would purposely go in where the religious leaders could see Him and would do something against what they held piously dear. He tried to get them to see the laws were made to aid people instead of burden and condemn them. He wanted them to see that His Father's motive was Love. God really loves us. God loves you reader. God loves me. It made people mean then, it makes us mean now. Religion does not know or value love; only works and comparisons. Religions' companions are pride, arrogance, haughtiness, racism, wars, murder and the like.

So why did Jesus come? Sacrifices atone for offenses. People who are involved in witchcraft and Satanism and secret societies understand this. Blood sacrifice is the most powerful. God Himself put on the flesh of man so He could provide the sacrifice for our offense against Him. His standard is perfection, which is why religion is futile. Our only way in, is through His perfection, not our works. He Is the perfect sacrifice.

GOD'S MESSAGE OF LOVE

Hebrews 9:28- So Christ was sacrificed once to take away the sins of many; and he will appear a second time, not to bear sin, but to bring salvation to those who are waiting for him.

Ephesians 5:2- And walk in the way of love, just as Christ loved us and gave himself up for us as a fragrant offering and sacrifice to God.

Titus 2:14- Who gave himself for us to redeem us from all wickedness and to purify for himself a people that are his very own, eager to do what is good.

THE CONVERSATION

The conversation is something that probably only near death experiencers will understand. Let me try to explain. The conversation that God began with me in my NDE is continuous.

He said to me "I have no condemnation for you...your life is not yours to take..."

Some months later, He said, "you let them know I Am a loving Father..." When He said that, it wasn't another dialogue; it was still the same conversation from months before in our time.

I used to teach bible classes and sometimes preach. I used to mock people who talked about God's love. I was so religious. In a way, His admonishment to me is a loving rebuke. So, dear reader-God is a loving Father. He loves you more than you can ever dream of loving your own children. Receive His love. Know He is for you.

I know this may sound crazy; I'm sure this whole book sounds crazy to some. I'm not afraid of nor am I ashamed of being called crazy.

Once I asked Him, "when did I come to know You?" I never remember a time in my life when I didn't believe God was there. He showed me the time when I was five years old going to the front of the church with my brother Dwight. This was still in the same conversation even though it was months later.

God is so Good. When I was in church as a youngster just counting Melchezideks, He was faithful. God lives in eternity. We live in time. When He speaks to us, we move to His realm, on His terms. I'm still trying to hear back from Him on the Powerball numbers.

GOD'S MESSAGE OF LOVE

Seems like dying, teach us bout livin'

Makes you preciate the chances

     you been givin'

Lose now and again-but sometime uze win

Yep Sometimes dying teach us bout livin'

Choose this way or the other

But weez all has trials one way or another

Trick is learning to love each other

Worry so much bout what we aint got

Heck, even a butterfly got spots

Whether you notice daze pretty o not

Oh yeah, sometimes dying teach us bout livin'

Who knew this long road could be a

Crystal stairway to Heaven…

ABOUT THE AUTHOR

Victor Hicks was born and raised in Kansas City, Kansas in the 1960s. He has been a deputy sheriff in his hometown for 20 years. He was brought up in traditional churches and is now ordained in a non-denominational organization. He is married with 3 grown children, 3 stepchildren and 5 grandchildren.

*After having two **Near Death Experiences**, he knew God wanted him to communicate what he'd seen and learned. Hopefully this book will be a blessing to its readers.*

Deputy Sheriff, Ordained Minister and now Author,

Victor Hicks

Made in the USA
Middletown, DE
12 March 2025

72561735R00069